CW01502307

How to Do Business in China

"A specter is haunting the world, the specter of China. Engage this exhilarating force!"

"There lies a sleeping dragon [China].
Let him sleep, for when he awakens,
he will shake the world."
—Attributed to Napoleon

The dragon has truly awakened from its slumber. . . .

How to Do Business in China

✔ 24 Lessons in Engaging the Dragon

NICK DALLAS

New York Chicago San Francisco Lisbon
London Madrid Mexico City Milan New Delhi
San Juan Seoul Singapore Sydney Toronto

Copyright © 2008 by McGraw-Hill, Inc. All rights reserved.
Printed in the United States of America. Except as permitted
under the United States Copyright Act of 1976, no part of this
publication may be reproduced or distributed in any form or by
any means, or stored in a database or retrieval system, without
prior written permission of the publisher.

1 2 3 4 5 6 7 8 9 0 DOC/DOC 0 9 8

ISBN: 978-0-07-159723-4
MHID: 0-07-159723-9

This publication is designed to provide accurate and authorita-
tive information in regard to the subject matter covered. It is
sold with the understanding that the publisher is not engaged
in rendering legal, accounting, or other professional service. If
legal advice or other expert assistance is required, the services
of a competent professional person should be sought.
    —*From a Declaration of Principles Jointly Adopted by a
    Committee of the American Bar Association and a
    Committee of Publishers and Associations*

McGraw-Hill books are available at special quantity discounts
to use as premiums and sales promotions, or for use in corporate training programs. To contact a representative, please visit
the Contact Us pages at www.mhprofessional.com.

This book is printed on acid-free paper.

Contents

How to Do Business in China

✔ How to do business in China

While the terminology may vary, whether it's embracing the market or socialism with "Chinese characteristics," nothing changes the fact that when it comes to modern-day global business, China is the biggest and most spectacular story in town. In a relatively short period of time, a country perceived as an economic backwater for most of the twentieth century has now emerged as an economic power-house and leading global player. Some aspects of its rise—massive investments in infrastructure projects, breakneck industrialization, and export-led manu-facturing growth—mirror previous Asian stellar economies, but its potentially colossal domestic market adds an unparalleled dimension.

China's rise is a watershed event that has trans-formed the global landscape. Pundits have dubbed the twenty-first century as the Chinese Century. For short-term projections, very few reasons exist to doubt this evaluation. Emboldened by more than two decades of uninterrupted, near double-digit economic growth, the China juggernaut will continue to maintain its momentum in the years ahead. Foreign firms are voting with their feet and pouring in billions of investment dollars as they seek part of the action.

If your firm is looking at reducing its cost structure or expanding beyond its national market, flirting with China is almost inevitable. Although there's no substitute for being on the ground, this book aims to provide some basic guidelines in dealing with this challenge and to give exposure to some of the principal issues.

"China is making up for lost time with unequalled energy and determination."

☐ Ignorance is bliss

☑ Better read than dead

Knowledge is power and ignorance isn't bliss. Don't just swallow the hype about China and repeat well-rehearsed clichés; don't accept the newspaper headlines uncritically. Convince yourself of the China story. Apart from being one of the oldest civilizations, China has had a tumultuous twentieth century marred by devastating wars, civil strife, and abrupt societal changes. And, for the last two-and-a-half decades, China has experienced economic reform and its associated consequences at a relentless pace. Most Westerners don't have the appropriate background or life experience to appreciate what such changes can have on the psyche of a nation and its people.

The China story might be unfolding, but to understand it, you must try to appreciate the context. Read widely about China across all disciplines:

history, politics, economics, culture, literature, and so on. You'll be better off for it. Once on the ground, what might have been initially interpreted as inconsequential or unexplained events and experiences will now have new meaning and appreciation as a result of your background reading.

Make an effort to understand China's past, especially the twentieth century. As China becomes more prominent in global affairs and news articles proliferate, you won't be able to properly appraise these stories without being familiar with China's past.

These days, it's amazing what random word searches on the Web can reveal. Look up articles on the post-Mao period when economic reform was introduced. Understanding this period, as well as the timing and motives of policies introduced, can give you insights on what future changes might be in store.

Visit blog sites dedicated to doing business in China. Expose yourself to the debates, controversies, and issues. Opinions will be diverse, but you'll become better informed.

Seek out business-case studies of firms that have done business in China. Quite a sizeable literature base is emerging in this area. Although every firm and venture is different and the business landscape is changing daily in China, these case studies may give forewarnings on issues, problems, and opportunities that may arise. Why repeat the mistakes of others and why not be attuned to how matters might evolve?

Arm yourself with an arsenal of knowledge on China and consider it a never-ending learning process.

- Being better informed increases the likelihood of making correct decisions as risk is reduced.
- The Internet has made access to information amazingly convenient; take advantage of it.

"Study the past if you would define the future."
—Confucius

"Life is finite, while knowledge is infinite."
—Zhuang Zi

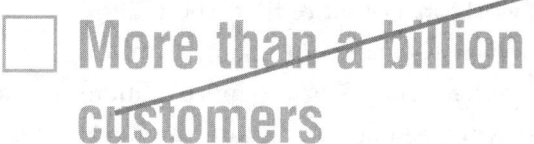

☑ China is not a monolithic market

"**M**ore than a billion customers" is the standard catchphrase used to lure foreign investors to China. China's population base increases annually by more than 10 million inhabitants; that's larger than the size of most nation-states.

China is by no means a single, monolithic, continental-size market. It's made up of a series of diverse regions of varying levels of development and peculiarities, all requiring their own market entry strategy. China's own nation-size provinces contain an array of local markets, all with their own business practices, traditions, methods of local protectionism, and degrees of entrepreneurship.

China has almost 100 cities of nearly one million or more inhabitants. Adding to this complexity is a transient workforce of more than 100 million, a vast pool of low-cost workers of mainly rural origin, in constant search of work in the more-affluent urban centers driving China's ambitious modernization. China is rapidly urbanizing, an inevitable trend with economic development. Within a decade or so, China's urban population will overtake the rural sector in size.

How do you tackle such a fragmented market with its numerous geographically and economically distinct submarkets? A large population doesn't imply a billion-plus potential customers. They still need to have the disposable income to purchase your product. Huge wealth disparities exist in China, not only among individuals, but also among regions. The Special Economic Zones and coastal provinces are by far wealthier and better endowed with infrastructure than their inland counterparts. Although living standards have improved substantially, average household incomes and consumption still remain quite low in rural and inland areas.

You should not be fazed by this "hyper-diversity." It just further reinforces the need for meticulous planning, and careful and fastidious research before entering the market. The more obvious, but often saturated, coastal areas that have a much higher average annual household income might not be your ideal entry point. Second- and third-tier cities might be worth looking at. Don't rule out more remote and inland provinces, whose advantages could be less competition and more accommodating local governments keen to attract investment, preserve local jobs, and maximize fiscal revenues.

Having acquired an understanding of China's fragmented domestic market and its economic geography, a firm must then have a strategy to address the following four themes:

- What are its goals and aspirations in China's domestic market?
- What segments of the domestic market will be targeted?
- How will it win market share in those chosen markets?
- What capabilities must be in place before moving in?

"China is not a homogeneous market of 1.3 billion people. Local knowledge is the key."

☐ ~~All you need is a book on etiquette~~

☑ **Get the cultural stuff right**

It's simply common sense when in any new environment to familiarize yourself with the local conditions and be conscious of local etiquette. The old adage—when in Rome, do as the Romans do—holds true. It's also true that common decency, which is a fairly universal prescribed trait, will get you through in most instances. As a foreigner, you're also more likely to be given the benefit of the doubt by your hosts. However, behaving arrogantly, being inconsiderate, and having a condescending attitude don't go down well and this isn't only true in China.

An essential cultural constituent of the Chinese national psyche is maintaining face. It bestows upon the individual a sense of honor and personal dignity in the eyes of their peers. Foreigners should take great care and make sure they don't unintentionally offend their Chinese counterparts, thus harming their chances of any business collaboration. This can easily occur because of cultural perceptions on what constitutes harmless comments and behavior or attempts at humor.

Culture is like an iceberg. The easy-to-see tip is the visible aspects of etiquette and behavior. Getting to know the larger, below-the-surface chunk of the iceberg containing the invisible aspects of culture such as values, traditions, attitudes, and beliefs is the challenge. Cultural myopia has caused so many companies, most unsuspectingly, to hit this iceberg, leading to countless stories of commercial failure.

Underestimating the need for cross-cultural awareness is an esy mistake to make. One must first be culturally fluent in their own culture before they can attempt to understand someone else's. Obtaining this cultural awareness through observation, self-reflection, and, more importantly, through face-to-face experience is vital in doing business successfully.

In general terms, Chinese and Western cultures are diametrically opposed in many dimensions: directness of speech, hierarchy, consensus, and individualism are only a few.

Gaining greater awareness of these cultural differences, while simultaneously exploring cultural similarities, can help you communicate more effectively.

- Cultural differences must first be understood and acknowledged before they are managed. In confusing situations, ask yourself how is culture shaping the reactions of the parties involved?
- If we show no knowledge of another's culture, its members have little incentive to establish ties of trust with us.
- Chinese is a high-context culture. Chinese people will assume those taking part in exchanges have the cultural and contextual background to interpret correctly what is being implied.
- Consider providing cross-cultural training for managers and staff.

"Despite popular beliefs to the contrary, the single greatest barrier to business success is the one erected by culture."

—Edward T. Hall and Mildred Reed Hall

☐ ~~Anyone will do to get started~~

☑ **Find the right partner**

Whether a foreign firm enters China as a wholly owned foreign enterprise or through a joint-venture arrangement, probably the single most important decision it can make that can have the greatest bearing on its successful entry is its choice of partner(s). Choosing the right partner can save a lot of grief long-term and provide a formidable advantage in kick-starting operations.

This is no easy and straightforward process. The requisite time and money should be spent on research, negotiations, and conducting due diligence. Seek diverse opinions, commission reports, and carry out local research. Cast your net widely before coming up with a short list of candidates.

17

On the one hand, be convinced that your prospective partner is suitable. Feel comfortable that they can handle your products. Seek assurances on the effectiveness and reach of their distribution networks. Visit their facilities. Talk to their employees, clients, and competitors. Develop a feel for the extent of their capabilities. Will dealing with you expose them to any conflict of interest vis-à-vis their existing obligations? Question them exhaustively about their market knowledge. Can you agree on common goals and how to achieve them? Do you agree on future directions?

On the other hand, this is a two-way street. Be prepared for a reciprocal set of demands by your partner. How will you handle requests for technology transfer or possible access to your home market?

The right partner can accelerate penetration of local markets based on their business links and experience of the operating environment. They should be able to assist in maintaining compliance with local rules and regulations, and also mediating with government authorities whenever necessary.

In the long run, having a reliable local partner and developing a degree of mutual trust and dependability can be a critical determinant in your success or failure in the Chinese marketplace.

- In markets that are difficult, complex, and lack transparency, a suitable local partner is often the difference between success and failure.
- Avoid short cuts. Spend the necessary time and devote sufficient resources in making an informed choice.

"If you don't find the right partner you could be lying in the same bed but dreaming different dreams."

—Chinese proverb

☐ China has joined the
WTO

☑ Don't expect a level playing field

Don't be lulled into a sense of false security by China's huge and ever-expanding domestic market. Its size is no guarantee for success. Competition can be fierce and brutal. On its present trajectory, China's economy is on track to surpass the size of the U.S. economy in the next few decades. This means every global player who has a significant presence in their industry sector will see it as their duty to be in China. If this isn't enough, ignore existing and yet-to-emerge local competitors at your peril.

Adding to competitive pressures are product surpluses that can quickly develop in Chinese markets as a result of overcapacity. In many instances, local competitors, often with access to low-cost capital and government encouragement, can enter a sector, exerting further downward pressure on prices. Once sluggish state-owned enterprises are under pressure to lift their game. Local firms can be masters at cost innovation. With access to low-cost talent, the ability to take advantage of state assets and, in some cases, greater managerial autonomy than Western firms, they can cause severe disruption.

The Chinese domestic market has a long way to go before reaching a level of maturity where dominant players in a sector make healthy profits and rely more on marketing and branding initiatives than on price cuts. The domestic market is at a competitive phase where local firms won't hesitate to launch a price war, the logic being it first weeds out any struggling competitors, leading later to greater market share and profits through industry consolidation, and second, lower prices expand industry demand as Chinese consumers are very price-sensitive. You need to have a strategy to respond to a future price war; otherwise, look forward to becoming a Schumpeterian victim.

The government often has a proactive business role in China. It can deliberately encourage foreign entry into a sector to speed reform and stimulate modernization, while in other sectors, perceived as strategically important long term, it can foster the entry of local aspirants. China was accepted as a member of the World Trade Organization (WTO) in 2001. In the long run, this should create a more level playing field for foreign entrants as import tariffs are lowered, with some industries benefiting more than others. In the short term, expect delays and inconsistencies in the implementation of WTO accession requirements.

- Maintaining and reinforcing your competitive strengths is your best insurance in surviving, prospering, and navigating through this not-so-level playing field.
- The government occasionally shifts the goalposts in certain industries. Depending on the circumstances, this may or may not disadvantage the foreign firm.
- Local competitors have cost innovation advantages. Don't underestimate them.

"Know the enemy and know yourself; in a hundred battles you will never be in peril."
—Sun Tzu

☐ ~~Have to be there~~

☑ Look before you leap

An amalgamation of spectacular economic growth, political stability, and massive potential profits has set off a tidal wave of enthusiasm for China. Stoked by media frenzy, it could also reach tsunami-like proportions. Not a day goes by without some thrilling story about China, often involving enormous numbers and mind-defying projections. In business presentations on commercial opportunities in China, the most common feature on graphs is curves rising exponentially. Almost everything about China appears to have a "bigger than Ben Hur" format—all the more reason to tread with caution.

No one is denying that China is going through an exhilarating and history-defining epoch where exciting business opportunities exist to pursue. China's achievements deserve the utmost admiration. Its bold reform agenda has not only delivered impressive and sustainable growth rates, but it also has delivered substantial reductions in poverty and unemployment for its people. The more pertinent question is this: Is China right for you? Is China right for your particular business at its specific stage of development? Does engagement with China complement your long-term plans: is there a strategic fit? Should alternative options and strategies be evaluated?

Don't succumb to China's appeal as a result of the herd mentality and global hype! Another prevailing attitude is that the Chinese business environment is so unique and opaque that information is unreliable, so it's best to enter the market without it and learn as you go along. This is foolhardy. Every attempt should be made to conduct due diligence before entering the market. In some cases, it might be difficult and there might be a significant financial cost involved, but it's worth it. Others enter the market on the expectation that with rising affluence and improved living standards, pent-up demand by Chinese consumers who are voracious savers will be unleashed.

Entering the market might also be the right strategy provided some fine-tuning takes place. Is your product suitable in its present format? Does it need tweaking and adjustment to Chinese conditions?

Asking the right questions is the key to determine correctly if China is right for your business.

- Don't enter China with the "everyone is there, we can't be left behind" attitude. You must have the right reasons.
- China abounds with opportunities for failure. Do your homework.
- Although China may be a huge and growing market, that fact doesn't guarantee profitability for any venture.

"The cautious seldom err."

—Confucius

"When you want to test the depths of a stream, don't use two feet."

—Chinese proverb

☑ Have a vision

Leadership and vision are intertwined, as are their fortunes. A vision has to be articulated by a leader. The leader is the one who sets the pace in achieving a vision by motivating and inspiring others. Where no vision exists, an organization can never reach its full potential. Numerous firms survive on the "if it ain't broke, there's no need to fix it" mentality. A false sense of comfort comes from repeating what works. If compelled, they might introduce the occasional improvement, but for the most part, they feel comfortable being reactive rather than proactive. Firms only become better when they are exposed to competitive pressures, and they are made to rethink their processes and operations.

Vision is about daring not to be complacent, and setting ambitious goals and challenges. It's about instilling belief and empowering employees to surpass those seemingly high hurdles. It gives purpose to a firm and its employees.

How will engagement with China impact on the vision of your firm? Its size enables you to think big. Where do you see your firm situated 10–15 years from now in the context of your China strategy? Those firms that will be successful in China have a vision and are shaping it every day. They're not there content to simply have a toehold in the marketplace. So many variables exist in doing business in China, and some are more controllable than others. Without a vision to propel them forward and guide direction, abrupt changes to these variables can easily sidetrack and derail firms from their mission.

- Vision is not a dream; vision is reality that has yet to come into existence.
- Instill belief of your vision in your employees because it is easier to follow a path if you believe that path leads to somewhere meaningful. Demonstrate how your vision links into a larger vision of China's future.
- Vision is about holding on to a clear agenda, while being unfazed by side issues.

"Vision is perhaps our greatest strength . . . it has kept us alive to the power and continuity of thought through the centuries, it makes us peer into the future and lends shape to the unknown."

—Li Ka Shing (Chairman of Hutchison Whampoa)

☐ Analyze things in a one-dimensional framework

☑ Analyze things in multidimensional and paradoxical frameworks

Western thought is noted for its strengths in categorization and analysis, whereas Eastern thought is noted for its integrative and encompassing nature. A common Western approach to solving complex problems is to deconstruct them into smaller constituent parts, and then solve the individual components. This approach may not work in China when it comes to understanding business matters, as often the components can be both interrelated and interdependent. Understanding China requires a more holistic approach based on a multidimensional framework. You must be conscious of the social and political, as well as economic, content to business in China. You must be knowledgeable enough and flexible enough to adapt to the Chinese environment.

One of the strengths of Chinese business ways is the ability to recognize and meet the needs of a wide variety of stakeholders. In making a decision, the Chinese official, bureaucrat, intermediary, or businessperson could be trying to satisfy multiple agendas (personal, social, political, and economic) and appease numerous parties.

China is also a land of contradictions. You might wonder how the Chinese can simultaneously espouse Confucian ideals, employ socialist phraseology, and embrace market forces. Aren't they opposing belief systems? Well, quite easily: by emphasizing and promoting the positive features and virtues of them all with the aim of achieving the best of all worlds. Appreciating things within a paradoxical framework is embedded in Chinese culture as a result of the influence of Taoist thought that embodies the harmony of opposites and striving for balance.

- Be observant and keep an open mind. The seemingly illogical on the surface might be logical after all.

- Learn to tolerate ambiguity; otherwise, you may jump to conclusions too quickly.
- In terms of webs of interlinking relationships, the Chinese have become masters at traversing through a socioeconomic and political landscape replete with contradictions.

"In an organizational and cultural context more can be gained by seeking to leverage rather than subdue opposite forces. Integrating potentially conflicting opposites into a harmonized whole, rather than sidelining them as inconsistencies, can unleash great opportunity."

☐ Irrational exuberance

☑ Expect setbacks, have a plan B

For quite a significant period of time, especially in the nineties, China was frequently portrayed as a black hole that swallowed up capital and technology with questionable benefits and poor returns on investments. Companies entered the market seduced by the numbers and got badly burned. Some cases can be attributed to bad preparation and overexuberance; in others, unexpected developments derailed projects. Companies relaxed their investment performance criteria for the sake of being one of the first to get a foothold in the market, hoping that, eventually, things would turn out favorably in the long run. The most common business story in the media was about joint ventures with misaligned partners having failed or not having lived up to expectations.

The early years were also difficult as numerous protectionist barriers and regulatory obstacles were still in place. Broad and rigid market-access restrictions affected many industry sectors and business activities. Many companies stuck it through, learned from their mistakes, lobbied for changes, adjusted their strategies, and, today, are key players. Others simply packed their bags, writing it off as an expensive failed exercise.

Today, the dynamics and nature of the debate have changed: business stories are more positive, and foreign companies are making money. If this weren't the case, China wouldn't be attracting the record levels of foreign direct investment that it has over the last few years.

Furthermore, joint ventures aren't the most common way to enter China. After changes to investment rules in 1998, an increasing number of companies are setting up as wholly foreign-owned enterprises, giving them more autonomy and control of their operations. This lack of control was a serious impediment in the past.

The moral of the story is this: China can be a rewarding but, simultaneously, a frustrating place to do business. Expect setbacks, be psychologically prepared for them as they're part of the learning process in any business venture. Meanwhile, don't go into the marketplace without a plan B. Have a fallback position if things go sour, even if this means packing your bags in a worst-case scenario.

- Develop plans to respond to potentially negative scenarios. Don't get caught unprepared.
- Having a setback isn't necessarily the issue because unexpected things happen all the time in business. The bigger problem is not learning from the setback.

"Our greatest glory is not in never falling, but in rising every time we fall."

—Confucius

☐ PRC (People's Republic of China)

☑ PRC (Patience, Relationship, Contract)

The adage "patience is a virtue" carries great weight when doing business in China. Without exercising the required patience in cultivating relationships, there's no chance any contracts will be signed. The reverse is equally true. No signed contract will be adhered to unless you invest the time in relationship building, and that requires patience.

Your Chinese partners will place more value on trusted relationships than on legal documents.

That's not to say that contracts aren't important. One must pay attention to the details and content of contracts. After all, contracts do entail minimum benchmarks for performance expectations. However, ideally, you don't want to be involved in legal disputes over nonfulfillment of contract terms, especially in an environment where the legal framework is still evolving.

An old Chinese puzzle asks how does one change an iron bar into a needle? The answer is by striking the iron bar over and over again ad infinitum. The moral of the story is that patience, perseverance, tenacity, and repetition are values to be admired in business. These types of values, associated with long-term thinking and commitment, are what it takes to build trust and maintain a strong relationship.

In Western business practice, a strong build-up of transactions usually ensures that a business relationship develops because a track record of successful interaction has occurred. Oppositely, Chinese businesspeople prefer that a trusted relationship with prospective business partners develops on a personal level first before commercial transactions can take place. The latter, no doubt, requires more patience.

- Patience is pivotal and will be rewarded in the long run.
- Chinese people like doing business face-to-face, a more time-consuming method that requires greater patience. Phone and e-mail aren't the same.

"It does not matter how slowly you go as long as you do not stop."

—Confucius

"Patience and the mulberry leaf become a silk robe."

—Old Chinese proverb

☐ All you ~~need is~~ a good product

☑ Kiss cadres, but embrace customers

Some basic fundamentals of business do not change the world over. Business is ultimately about satisfying customers' needs by providing them with suitable products and services at prices they consider reasonable and affordable, while making a profit for the firm-provider. Losing sight of your customers' needs is the beginning of a firm's decline.

With this is mind, a firm must always be vigilant: markets change, new products and competitors emerge, and even customer loyalty can waver. For survival and longevity reasons, customer needs and producing desirable products and services should take center stage in any firm's agenda. In the background, though, a firm also needs to deal with bureaucracy and cultivate relationships on many levels, as this is the nature of doing business in China.

China's bureaucracy isn't homogeneous. On business matters, more and more decision-making powers are being devolved to regional, provincial, and municipal authorities. This decentralization of powers and functions has given local authorities tremendous discretionary powers when it comes to adjudicating on economic matters. This is also responsible for regional disparities in approval processes because it leaves the door open for selective implementation and enforcement, hence creating a not-so-level playing field and providing a springboard for local protectionism.

A nascent legal and regulatory environment has also significantly increased the scope for inconsistent decisions as local bureaucrats are now responsible for enforcing often-vague laws and regulations. Rules and laws might be in abundance in China. What's insufficient are reliable and consistent interpretative processes. This makes the fostering of good relations with government authorities essential.

With time, we would expect a more transparent and mature legal and regulatory framework to emerge, giving investors greater predictability and more consistent outcomes.

It's important not to forget that:

- Customers are your lifeblood. Don't lose sight of your customers at any cost.
- Play the game and work with government circles. You need these relationships with authorities to navigate through the regulatory maze.
- You cannot solve a provincial problem by going to Beijing.

"Local authorities could be the barrier preventing you [from] reaching your customers. It pays to be on good terms with them."

☐ ~~IPR protection is a lost cause~~

☑ Protect your crown jewels

It is no secret that counterfeiting and trademark, patent, and copyright infringement are rampant in China. China's poor record in upholding intellectual property rights (IPR) protection is considered one of the biggest obstacles to business, and there's no quick and easy fix to the problem. Foreign firms have forgone billions of dollars of lost revenue as a result of these widespread violations. This is a common sore point in trade negotiations. Numerous foreign firms are fearful of exposing their patented technologies to the Chinese market.

China is cracking down on IPR abuses. As a signatory to the WTO, it is obliged to do so. However, implementation and enforcement of regulations often fall short. While suing successfully is possible, litigation costs are high, whereas the fines and penalties imposed on offending firms are rather modest. Given time, compliance will definitely improve, not only as a result of greater international pressure, but it also will be demanded more and more by local Chinese firms with global ambitions. Otherwise, they will be unable to cultivate their brands and compete globally.

Chinese firms are spending more on research and development to spur on product innovation, as well as to move up the value chain where the profit margins are higher. Many are at the stage where they can compete internationally in areas of software and high technology, where IPR protection is essential for success. Innovation is the key, not only to higher margins, but also for companies to remain competitive in the long term and to have a global reach. This can only occur if IPR protection is afforded to innovators.

Companies concerned about their products being reverse-engineered should have a strategy in place if this eventuates. It may involve building more sensitive components offshore and leaving final assembly in China. Other strategies could be keeping critical technologies out of China or embedding security features.

No easy or straightforward solution exists, but having IPR safeguards in place should be part of any firm's entry strategy. Meanwhile, China needs to be continually engaged on issues of intellectual property through a variety of channels.

- Register whatever you can and wherever you can in China.
- Conduct regular inspections of the market for infringements and don't hesitate to sue if need be.
- The ability of China's court system to enforce judgments and awards on IPR matters is improving, but it still has a long way to go. There are cases of Chinese firms suing other local firms.

"Quite often a firm's intellectual property is their most significant competitive advantage; fervent efforts should be made to defend this."

☑ Chinese negotiating style

Negotiating business in China can be more akin to playing chess than deal-making: it's often portrayed as protracted guerrilla warfare. Many books that mention the topic treat it as a strategic philosophy, drawing frequent parallels with the content of *Thirty-Six Stratagems*, a compilation of ancient military maxims, and Sun Tzu's classic *The Art of War*. Significant cultural differences and perceptions exist on how negotiations should be carried out. Negotiations have been known to fail because of a lack of cultural awareness, rather than the absence of common ground. Often the key to success is knowing how to navigate these differences in cultural values.

Chinese negotiators use time more consciously than their Western counterparts. They are skilled at maximizing their role as hosts by controlling the location and timing of meetings, the arrangement of agendas, and the pace of negotiations. Westerners have a tendency to be impatient and very goal-oriented, treating negotiations as simply a process to achieve their final goals, often the signing of contracts. The Chinese are more process-oriented and are often concerned with things not specifically outlined in contracts, such as intentions of good will and mutual understandings.

Westerners revere contracts as they clearly outline the specific obligations of the parties therein. For the Chinese, the signing of contracts is simply the beginning of a relationship, and the contracts are open to revisiting and renegotiation. The understanding and friendship between the firms are more highly valued.

The key to successful negotiations is getting the Chinese counterpart to disclose what they really want to achieve from the deal. Formal negotiations might not reveal this if there's too much emphasis on sizing up each other and other mind games. However, in more relaxed and informal settings, for example, banquets where individual negotiators can interact on a personal level, these details may emerge. If key decision makers come to an understanding outside the formal process, the deal often proceeds.

Remember, with negotiations:

- Come thoroughly prepared, just as your counterparts will be.
- Allow plenty of time; painstaking patience may be required.
- Give due recognition to protocol, procedure, and precedence.
- Read up on Chinese negotiating tactics.

"Sometimes it is better not to take a straight road to your destination."

—Chinese proverb

"He who knows the art of the direct and indirect approach will be victorious. Such is the art of maneuvering."

—Sun Tzu

~~English is the global language of business~~

☑ **Mandarin is king**

Don't rely on getting by with only English in China. Its use is becoming more widespread, staggering numbers are studying it, and you'll come across countless individuals with varying degrees of fluency; however, Mandarin rules supreme.

China has seven major language groups of which Mandarin is the largest. More than 400 dialects are spoken in mainland China alone. The Mandarin dialect of Beijing has official language status in China. Mandarin is spoken by more than 90 percent of the population and it's quite common for most to speak some other dialect, often reflecting their birthplace origins.

Never underestimate the importance of language skills as you do business in China. While downplaying their significance is common, the main priorities of business are to make money and generate profits. The "language stuff" can be left to interpreters and bilinguals—after all, that's why they're hired.

Interpretation and translation are professional skills. Hire professionals where needed; being bilingual may not be enough. In legal and contract matters, knowledge of Mandarin assumes even greater importance. It's critical that definitions are not lost in translation because Mandarin overrules any English definition.

When conveying information in product literature, misleading messages could be sent out if you aren't conversant in the subtleties of both languages and fully aware of the cultural context.

Devoting some time to acquire rudimentary knowledge and basic expressions in Mandarin is time well invested. Doing this can reduce the distance between your world and that of your Chinese business partners. You'll be both appreciated and respected for your efforts.

Language acquisition can also provide important cultural insights and further assist you in conducting business.

- If you have any expatriate staff, make it obligatory that they attend Chinese language courses as part of their training.

- When language is at the center of important tasks, hire professionals. This is cheaper in the long run.
- Don't confuse language ability with business or management competence.

"Foreign language competency might be considered a 'soft skill,' but in negotiating or writing up of contracts, it can be the difference between a successful or failed deal."

☑ **Have a realistic business plan**

Before getting involved in China, make sure your project is viable by having a realistic business plan. An investment project should be able to stand on its own merit. Don't rely on subsidies, waived fees, or other promised incentives to make the project viable. These should be treated as a bonus and not factored in as contributing to a project's viability.

What makes a business plan realistic is the quality of inputs. This is tricky as any piece of information on business prospects in China can't always be taken on face value and should be treated with caution. It might be more important to get the strategy aspect of the business plan correct first. Later, the elaboration of the numbers and calculations can follow. A suitable strategy should involve finding the right contacts on the ground, and then deciding on a location and what market to target in advance. Without this information in place, the business plan becomes quite speculative, making it difficult to remain within its financial parameters.

Don't skimp on doing the necessary research and obtaining the details to make your business plan credible. It's tempting to treat China as a long-term project and accept that profit may have to be sacrificed in the early years. Set performance benchmarks and aim to achieve profitability in the short term as anything could happen in the long run.

Once a business plan has been approved, its implementation must be approached with conviction. A halfhearted approach will lead to a quick demise as China isn't a market for the faint-hearted. Trusted and capable people must be on the ground, managing the project. Remote control management is unsuitable.

Formulating a business plan requires:

- Sound understanding of the business environment.
- Clarity on the market and business opportunities at hand.
- Realistic expectations aligned with performance benchmarks.

"The general who wins the battle makes many calculations in his temple before the battle is fought. The general who loses makes but few calculations beforehand."

—Sun Tzu

☐ Whatever it takes

☑ Observe the local rules and regulations

Deng Xiaoping's famous "the-end-justifies-the-means" dictum, "It doesn't matter whether the cat is black or white, as long as it catches the mouse," doesn't apply in this situation. Operating within the law is the right way to do business in China. It doesn't pay to overlook the local rules and regulations to achieve the desired results.

The sudden lure of wealth deriving from the transition of a centrally planned economy to a more market-oriented one throws up countless opportunities for corrupt practices. Whether it's bribes, kickbacks, fraud, or outright theft, the mere fact that more money is floating around means temptation for corrupt behavior abounds. Foreign firms entering China should refrain from partaking in such practices. Apart from being illegal and violating their company's charter, corrupt practices have a tendency to come back and haunt the firm or individual involved.

The argument is often that competitors are getting ahead as a result of such unscrupulous practices. What's wrong with the occasional "facilitation payment," since everyone is doing it? Firms can do immense harm to their long-term prospects in the Chinese market if such practices are uncovered and they become tainted.

There's a paradox of performance regarding foreign firms in China. The outside world is hearing about China's spectacular economic achievements, so tremendous expectations exist to deliver extraordinary economic growth, whereas reality on the ground is much tougher. This imbalance of expectations and performance pressures can push firms into taking shortcuts, resulting in the violation of local rules and regulations.

Another source of frustration for foreign firms is regulatory roadblocks. There's an inconsistent application of Chinese laws at different government levels. The temptation is to use irregular means to overcome such barriers. We can only hope that with time, greater openness will shore up investor confidence, so such hurdles can be cleared with greater bureaucratic transparency and administrative predictability.

- Abide by the local rules and regulations at all times if you want peace of mind.
- Avoid all forms of questionable payment.
- Avoid prohibitive agreements.

"With coarse rice to eat, with water to drink, and my bended arm for a pillow—I have still joy in the midst of these things. Riches acquired by unrighteousness are to me as a floating cloud."

—Confucius

☐ All answers are to be found inside China

☑ Investigate diaspora links

In broad terms the Chinese diaspora comprises some 60 million people with claims of Chinese ancestry living outside mainland China. Depending on the context, Hong Kong, Taiwan, and Macau can also fall into this category. Although spread worldwide, overseas Chinese mostly live in Southeast Asia, where they dominate the business elites. In recent decades, greater numbers have been settling in such countries as Australia, the United States, and Canada. Their degree of cultural assimilation in their host society differs widely. What doesn't differ is their reputation as being business savvy, and having a strong work ethic and a strong propensity to save.

A significant proportion of foreign direct investment toward China emanates from the Chinese diaspora community. With the commencement of China's Open Door Policy, overseas Chinese were the dominant source of investment funds until the mid-1990s. They were some of the first investors to test mainland Chinese waters during this period, despite the inherent uncertainties. No doubt, cultural affinity expedited this process. Because of labor shortages and other local constraints in their home countries, China was seen as an ideal emerging low-cost location to relocate and expand their manufacturing operations. Also, more importantly, they had the financial nous, entrepreneurial experience, and an understanding of the Western mindset and business practices to identify and cultivate export markets for these manufactured goods. Simultaneously engaging in business with China gave them the opportunity to rediscover their ancestral links and reinvigorate their cultural awareness.

Interestingly, some of the biggest investors have been the Taiwanese, reinforcing the pragmatism and acumen that exists among businesspeople on both sides of the Taiwan Strait, despite the saber-rattling that occurs at government level.

Entering China might be facilitated through diaspora connections in your home country. Seek out Chinese business associations and chambers of commerce; there might be opportunities to leverage their knowledge and business links in China. When it comes to recruiting bilingual staff, again, your home territory might be the ideal recruiting ground.

- Answers to your China plans may be closer to home than you think.
- China's rapid modernization has been hastened and spearheaded by its ethnically linked, business-oriented diaspora funneling billions of investment dollars toward it.

"Chinese immigrants have settled in all corners of the globe, making them one of the most widespread of diaspora communities."

☑ Guanxi is part of the story

No book on doing business in China would be complete without mentioning "guanxi." *Guanxi* can be translated in a myriad of ways: contacts, connections, relationships, and trust. Cultivating guanxi is essential in any successful business venture. With time, this might diminish as China becomes more integrated with global markets and the business environment becomes more predictable. In the meantime, however, overlooking guanxi is short-sighted. Guanxi is often the lubricant in getting results because of a weak commercial legal system and a heavily laden bureaucracy. Personal contacts have been necessary to cut through this maze and opaqueness to get things done. Guanxi puts the value of relationships above transactions, but also comes with reciprocal obligations which, under certain circumstances, can become awkward.

For guanxi to be effective, it needs to be web-like. An extensive network of relationships with people at various levels in a wide range of organizations needs to be nurtured. In practical terms, guanxi is to be admired for its obstacle-removing and opportunity-creating potential.

Foreign businesses are often attracted to doing business in China as a result of its low labor costs and large domestic market, while underestimating the high transaction costs required in cultivating relationships.

The business climate in China is strongly skewed toward a business climate where relationships and reputations are highly valued. Unless a considerable amount of time is spent in building these relationships and establishing a strong and trustworthy reputation, progress will be slow.

- Guanxi can minimize the risks and frustration of doing business in China. It is vital to any successful business strategy.
- Doing business within guanxi circles can offer protection and certainty where legal protection is difficult to enforce.

"Guanxi represents a blurring of the personal and professional. People's sense of themselves is largely determined by their relationships with others and how they are perceived by others. That the social should overspill into the commercial shouldn't come as surprising."

☐ ~~Risk is unavoidable, accept it~~

☑ **Perform thorough risk analysis**

After getting over the euphoria and mystique of entering a market with a billion-plus potential consumers, sober reality attaches a high-risk premium to investing in China. Enormous opportunities come with enormous risks. One of the keys to doing business in China is being prepared to deploy appropriate measures and sufficient resources to mitigate this risk.

Outside your standard business risks that affect all companies in any competitive business environment, legal and regulatory risk are high in China. China isn't a mature market economy supported by a strong legal-judicial framework. China is a market-oriented or hybrid economy, which basically implies it's still a "work in progress" and all the players are trying to find their feet.

77

Other significant risks pertain to transparency and corporate governance issues. In a transition economy, conflicts of interest, fraud, and corruption are more pronounced in opaque business-operating conditions. Firms should have in place internal controls and staff-awareness programs that might detect and deter such practices. They should also consider external audits.

Although China does have corruption, it would be unfair to categorize it as rampantly corrupt. China is seriously cracking down on corruption. In any emerging market, realism dictates that corruption is part of the process of growing pains involved with investment. It's in China's best interest to clamp down on corruption and improve transparency if it wants to continue attracting the record levels of investment flows desired for continued modernization.

- Risk is involved with all investment decisions. Firms need to conduct appropriate due diligence on every facet of their business and closely monitor China's operating environment.
- Managing risk is an ongoing process requiring never-ending vigilance. There's no respite.

"The only thing certain and constant about China is uncertainty. Managing risk is about dealing with uncertainty and the unexpected."

"Water retains no constant shape. In warfare there are no constant conditions."

—Sun Tzu

☐ Business in China is different

☑The key business challenges remain the same

China is going through a monumental reform process with no equivalent in history. About turns, surprises, and even seismic shifts in policy are all part of the process. However, with time, China's economic maturity, its reliance on international trade and investment, its interconnectedness with the world economy, its ascension to the WTO, and its move toward global standards all point toward a convergence of business practices. Therefore, the principal concerns of firms entering the market are the traditional concerns of doing business anywhere in the world: how to get the strategy right, how to reach consumers, how to manage partners, and how to manage employees.

Getting the strategy right will be highly instrumental in getting off to a good start in the challenging China market. Good strategy comes with good intelligence. Good intelligence comes by having good people on the ground: people who know local markets, and people who understand the business and regulatory environment. If this isn't the case, be prepared to spend and seek professional help to uncover such market knowledge.

To be executed successfully, good strategy also needs good partners—partners who can direct consumers to your products. Good strategy is also about knowing your partners. Is communication frequent? Are your interests aligned? Do you know your partners' constraints?

Ultimately, people make businesses succeed or fail. Having the best product isn't sufficient if you don't have the right people in place to implement your strategy. The hiring, ongoing management, and development of your employees are extremely demanding and multifaceted tasks. The language issue further exacerbates the challenges.

Business in China is not too different after all.

■ Getting the right strategy and all the business basics in place should be the firm's main focus.

"Outside the China-specific issues facing any new entrant, the universal concerns of doing business daily and getting the basics right, remains the biggest challenge for any firm."

☐ Go with the flow

☑ Have a proactive government PR policy

During China's economic reform process, broad policy objectives and targets can easily be outlined. The difficult part is the implementation and working out of the policy details at different government levels, and then enshrining them in legislation. Multiple ministries may be involved, different industries have different issues and challenges, and then there are coordination and execution aspects. The challenges are enormous and perplexing, which is why this has been a gradual and trial-and-error process.

Calling in expert opinion, borrowing from successful overseas examples, and then adjusting for local conditions is no guarantee for success. This is just a starting point. Also, a huge gap exists between theory and practice. Legislation can be introduced, but quite a significant lag process occurs until citizens become familiar with it, and then embrace it in their decision making. China's authorities have shown a pragmatic and responsible streak during this era. When an economic policy or industry sector guidelines have been faltering, they've usually intervened to make changes to conserve investment flows and minimize any disruptions. Realpolitik has often triumphed over ideological and other concerns to turn around performance. This also means authorities don't ignore lobbying efforts by affected parties.

Regulatory frameworks are there to outline the rules of the game, but they need constant monitoring. At times, they can become ineffectual simply because of technological advances, bureaucratic inertia, or legislative roadblocks. In this context, it's important for firms to have a proactive government public relations policy to lobby for changes. It's also important to gain an understanding of what motivates key government decision makers and regulators. Higher levels of government are focused on China achieving its macro-level goals, which may complement your firm's long-term growth strategy.

In this lobbying process, firms should not hesitate to coordinate their activities with their embassy bureaus and relevant government trade bodies in their home countries.

- In your PR policy, highlight the overlap and compatibility of your company's goals with those of the nation.
- In fights with bureaucracy, take them to the highest level possible where officials are more likely to take China's larger interests into consideration.

"China is under the microscope of global investors; lobbying efforts don't go unnoticed. Its leaders are pragmatic and concerned about getting the big picture right, which means regular adjustments and fine-tuning of economic policy."

☐ Information is generally
reliable

☑ Never assume anything

Since the ascent of Deng Xiaoping to power until today, China has interchangably stumbled and soared through a massive and unprecedented trial-and-error reform process with the aim of modernizing its economy, revamping its institutions, and asserting its superpower credentials. During this period of profound transformation and fluidity, some legislation is made on the run and information flows are incomplete, making it difficult to understand the operating environment.

Seemingly objective facts obtained from different sources can appear both true and contradictory. In such instances, understanding the nature of the source is critical. Behind information could be a desire to achieve certain policy objectives, other goals of self-interest, or outright inaccuracies.

The reality of evolving China is not to rely on a single source of information. Seek information and opinions from a variety of sources. Having too much business information in such a fluctuating environment is impossible. The dissemination of information on commercial matters and industry statistics will improve with time as the economy matures, government bodies enhance their data collection capabilities, and more specialist information providers enter the market. Meanwhile, exercise caution in the short term.

The same can be said about human behavior: never assume anything. Get to know your counterparts well and don't become excessively overreliant on a handful of players. People change jobs and their roles change; influence can wane. Your Chinese partner or collaborator could be wearing many hats and trying to achieve numerous, albeit competing, objectives. Chinese people are not fazed by paradox. They consider it normal because, often, life is about balancing competing aims and achieving harmony.

When it comes to information:

- Carefully scrutinize your sources, and avoid single sources of information and informal assurances.
- Try and verify critical information at hand from alternative sources.

- Don't put all your eggs in one basket when it comes to relying on people. Have a range of contacts you can call on. Seek safety in numbers.

"An old dictum of caution, anything one cares to say about China is true; and so is the opposite. In China everything is possible, and everything is impossible."

☑ Enjoy the learning experience

There's no shortage of opinion on China, often simplistically polarized, from the alarmist and dire pessimistic to the overly optimistic. Is China a future threat or a welcoming counterbalancing force? The full spectrum of opinion can be found. The huge numbers appear to have caused a fatal attraction, making it impossible to ignore.

Will China be the expected El Dorado for foreign firms always eager to expand their reach and please their shareholders? Or, will it be another familiar emerging-market graveyard for investors as its economy overheats, overcapacities emerge, and boom turns to bust?

Will this "Workshop of the World" continue to keep the world out of recession by putting downward pressure on prices? Or, will its insatiable appetite for resources cause severe price distortions and supply imbalances?

In this maelstrom of economic and social change, what will happen to the environment as the Chinese consumers increase their consumption levels? Is modernization for China a Faustian bargain as pollution reaches unprecedented levels? Are there environmental constraints to China's phenomenal growth or will technology come forward and provide the necessary solutions?

China is not only growing, but it's steadily moving up the value-added scale. China is entering into higher margin, high-end products without deserting the low-end, low-margin, cutthroat sectors. With its export prowess and when its repertoire covers the entire product-quality spectrum, what impact will this have on industries across the globe?

As Chinese companies enter the global market, they are starting to buy up well-known companies overseas. This will become more common as China seeks to invest its financial largesse acquired through recurring trade surpluses. The acquisition trail also includes numerous natural resource companies, part of China's strategy to secure long-term supply links for raw materials necessary in its modernization drive. How will this trend affect global business and financial markets?

These are only some of the unanswered questions concerning China. Reading more on China makes you better informed, but it doesn't necessarily bring out greater clarity. Reading more simply exposes greater complexity and offers more permutations of how the future may evolve.

What happens in the twenty-first century is going to be highly determined by developments in China. As history unfolds, for those fortunate enough to be there to witness this monumental spectacle, simply savor the learning experience.

- In understanding China, there is no substitute for time, experience, and being on the ground doing business.
- Arguably, China is the most potent force shaping the twenty-first century.

"The once-sleeping giant has awoken and it's keen to regain its rightful place in global affairs."

☐ ~~Wait and see~~

☑ Just do it!

No amount of reading will fully prepare you for the challenges of doing business in China. At best, it will make you aware of basic blunders to avoid. Once all the necessary research, analysis, and preparatory work are done, you must then be on the ground to be exposed to the daily challenges and rigors of engaging the dragon. Those daily interactions with individuals, those daily responses in addressing expected and, even more important, unexpected issues, are the essence of the steep learning curve that must be embarked on. Being exposed to the daily machinations, frustrations, vagaries, and nuances of Chinese business life, apart from testing your resolve, can only enhance your understanding of Chinese society and business. These experiences, coupled with profound patience and unnerving stamina, will lay the groundwork for your future success.

For those firms that want to consider gaining a foothold in China, sooner is better than later. New entrants have more than two decades' experience of foreign involvement to reflect on. While early mover advantage might be too late for many, the challenge might be how to leapfrog existing industry leaders and set up new rules of engagement. Once on the ground, the market potential and local landscape can be better surveyed. Furthermore, you are also better positioned to articulate a vision and put pieces into place to capitalize on this opportunity.

China will continue its pace of frantic economic growth and reform in the short term. By no means is China a saturated market in numerous industry sectors. Changes to the country's financial structure and increased spending by its consumers will keep things buoyant for years to come. For many businesses, engagement with China is inevitable. Embrace the challenge, and expect it to be anything but a passive affair.

Make a start . . . take the plunge . . . just do it!

"A journey of a thousand miles begins with a single step."
—Lao Tzu

"Wheresover you go, go with all your heart."
—Confucius

"By three methods we learn wisdom: First, by reflection, which is noblest; second, by imitation, which is easiest; and third by experience, which is the bitterest."

—Confucius

"Doing business in China is about relationships, relationships, and relationships. Chinese like to do things on the personal level."

Sources and Suggested Readings

Tim Ambler, *Doing Business in China*, 2nd ed. (New York: Routledge Curzon, 2004).

Michael Backman and Charlotte Butler, *Big in Asia: 25 Strategies for Business Success* (New York: Palgrave Macmillan, 2002).

Laurence J. Brahm, *Doing Business in China: The Sun Tzu Way* (Boston: Tuttle Publishing, 2004).

Laurence J. Brahm, *Negotiating in China: 36 Strategies* (Singapore: Reed Academic Publishers, 1995).

Harold Chee and Chris West, *Myths About Doing Business in China* (New York: Palgrave Macmillan, 2005).

Ming-Jin Chen, *Inside Chinese Business: A Guide for Managers Worldwide* (Boston: Harvard Business School Press, 2003).

Tim Clissold, *Mr. China: A Memoir* (Sydney: Random House Australia, 2004).

Robert Collins and Carson Block, *Doing Business in China for Dummies* (Hoboken, NJ: Wiley Publishing, 2007).

Gavin Crombie, *The Way of the Dragon: A Guide for Australians Doing Business in China* (Melbourne: Wrightbooks, 2005).

Mia Doucet, *China in Motion: 17 Secrets to Slashing the Time to Production, Market, Profits in China, Japan, and South Korea* (London, ONT: Bankerman Press, 2004).

Pete Engardio, *Chindia: How China and India are Revolutionizing Global Business* (New York: McGraw-Hill, 2006).

Ted C. Fishman, *China Inc.: How the Rise of the Next Superpower Challenges America and the World* (London: Pocket Books, 2006).

Jeremy Haft, *All the Tea in China: How to Buy, Sell, and Make Money on the Mainland* (New York: Portfolio, 2007).

George T. Haley, Usha C. V. Haley, and Chin Tiong Tan, *The Chinese Tao of Business: The Logic of Successful Business Strategy* (Singapore: John Wiley & Sons Asia, 2004).

Harvard Business Review on Doing Business in China (Boston: Harvard Business School Publishing, 2004).

N. Mark Lam and John L. Graham, *China Now: Doing Business in the World's Most Dynamic Market* (New York: McGraw-Hill, 2006).

James Lord, *The Essential Guide for Buying from China's Manufacturers: The 10 Steps to Success* (Charleston: BookSurge Publishing, 2007).

James McGregor, *One Billion Customers: Lessons from the Front Lines of Doing Business in China* (London: Nicholas Brealey, 2005).

Sheila Melvin, *The Little Red Book of China Business* (Naperville, IL: Sourcebooks, Inc., 2007).

Ted Plafker, *Doing Business in China: How to Profit in the World's Fastest Growing Market* (New York: Warner Business Books, 2007).

Lucian W. Pye, *Chinese Negotiating Style: Commercial Approaches and Cultural Principles* (New York: Quorum Books, 1992).

Mike Saxon, *An American's Guide to Doing Business in China: Negotiating Contracts and Agreements; Understanding Culture and Customs; Marketing Products and Services* (Avon, MA: Adams Media Corporation, 2006).

Michael Yih-chung Shen, *How to Do Business in China* (Pittsburgh: Dorrance Publishing, 2004).

Oded Shenkar, *The Chinese Century: The Rising Chinese Economy and Its Impact on the Global Economy, the Balance of Power, and Your Job* (Upper Saddle River, NJ: Wharton School Publishing, 2006).

Donald Sull and Yong Wang, *Made in China: What Western Managers Can Learn from Trailblazing Chinese Entrepreneurs* (Boston: Harvard Business School Press, 2005).

Ernie Tadla, *How to Live & Do Business In China: Eight Lessons I Learned from the Communists* (Victoria BC: Trafford Publishing, 2007).

Ming Zeng and Peter J. Williamson, *Dragons at Your Door: How Chinese Cost Innovation Is Disrupting Global Competition* (Boston: Harvard Business School Press, 2007).

Linong Zhou, *China Business: Environment, Momentum, Strategies, and Prospects* (Singapore: Pearson Education Asia, 2006).

The McGraw-Hill Mighty Managers Handbooks

The Powell Principles
by Oren Harari (0-07-144490-4)

Details two dozen mission- and people-based leadership skills that have guided Colin Powell through his nearly half-century of service to the United States.

Provides a straight-to-the-point guide that any leader in any arena can follow for unmitigated success.

How Buffett Does It
by James Pardoe (0-07-144912-4)

Expands on 24 primary ideas Warren Buffett has followed from day one.

Reveals Buffett's stubborn adherence to the time-honored fundamentals of value investing.

The Lombardi Rules
by Vince Lombardi, Jr. (0-07-144489-0)

Presents more than two dozen of the tenets and guidelines Lombardi used to drive him and those around him to unprecedented levels of success.

Packed with proven insights and techniques that are especially valuable in today's turbulent business world.

The Welch Way

by Jeffrey A. Krames (0-07-142953-0)

Draws on the career of Jack Welch to explain how workers can follow his proven model.

Shows how to reach new heights in today's wide-open, idea-driven workplace.

The Ghosn Factor

by Miguel Rivas-Micoud (0-07-148595-3)

Examines the life, works, and words of Carlos Ghosn, CEO of *Nissan* and *Renault*.

Provides 24 succinct lessons that managers can immediately apply.

How to Motivate Every Employee

by Anne Bruce (0-07-146330-5)

Provides strategies for infusing your employees with a passion for the work they do.

Packed with techniques, tips, and suggestions that are proven to motivate in all industries and environments.

The New Manager's Handbook

by Morey Stettner (0-07-146332-1)

Gives tips for teaming with your employees to achieve extraordinary goals.

Outlines field-proven techniques to succeed and win the respect of both your employees and your supervisors.

The Sales Success Handbook

by Linda Richardson (0-07-146331-3)

> Shows how to sell customers—not by what you tell them, but by how well you listen to what they have to say.

> Explains how to persuasively position the value you bring to meet the customer's business needs.

How to Plan and Execute Strategy

by Wallace Stettinius, D. Robley Wood, Jr., Jacqueline L. Doyle, and John L. Colley, Jr. (0-07-148437-X)

> Provides 24 practical steps for devising, implementing, and managing market-defining, growth-driving strategies.

> Outlines a field-proven framework that can be followed to strengthen your company's competitive edge.

How to Manage Performance

by Robert Bacal (0-07-148439-8)

> Provides goal-focused, common-sense techniques to stimulate employee productivity in any environment.

> Details how to align employee goals and set performance incentives.

Managing in Times of Change

by Michael D. Maginn (0-07-148436-1)

> Helps you to understand and explain the benefits of change, while flourishing within the new environment.

> Provides straight talk and actionable advice for teams, managers, and individuals.

Leadership When the Heat Is On

by Danny Cox with John Hoover (0-07-148653-4)

Provides 24 practical lessons in high-performance management when under pressure.

Hands-on techniques for infusing your company with results-driven leadership during times of mergers, layoffs, and other organizational turmoil.